GIRL Talk

C. A. Plaisted
Illustrated by Chris Dickason

SAUNDERS
BOOK COMPANY

Illustrator: Chris Dickason
Editor: Lauren Taylor
Designer: Matthew Kelly

Consultants: John Rees and Kayla Jackson
John is a teacher, trainer, and educational consultant who works with schools, local governments and health workers across the United Kingdom. He is committed to supporting professionals who work for young people.

Kayla is a manager, trainer, and facilitator who works with communities, schools, and young people around the United States to ensure that they receive high-quality and accurate health information. She is dedicated to making sure that all young people are able to grow up safe and healthy in their communities.

Copyright © QEB Publishing, Inc. 2011

Published in 2011 by
Saunders Book Company
27 Stewart Road
Collingwood, ON Canada L9Y 4M7

ISBN 978-1-926853-91-8

Printed in China

A CIP record for this book is available from Library and Archives Canada.

Website information is correct at the time of going to press. However, the publishers cannot accept responsibility for information, links, or any other content of Internet websites or third-party websites.

This book is not intended to replace the advice of professional health care. It should be used as an additional resource only. Concerns about mental or physical health should always be discussed with a doctor or professional health-care provider.

CONTENTS

Puberty: What's That?

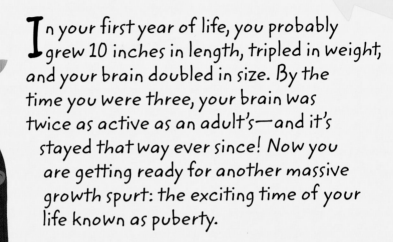

In your first year of life, you probably grew 10 inches in length, tripled in weight, and your brain doubled in size. By the time you were three, your brain was twice as active as an adult's—and it's stayed that way ever since! Now you are getting ready for another massive growth spurt: the exciting time of your life known as puberty.

The whole point of puberty is to get you to change from being a child to an adult.

The one thing you've got to remember is that puberty is different for everyone. What may happen to your best friend at 11 years old may not happen to you until you are 13 or even older. We are all so different! Have you got that? Promise? Good. Now let's start...

* finding out about the amazing things that are going to happen to you.
* putting your mind at rest about some of the things that are definitely not going to happen to you.
* dealing with the things that might happen as you grow up.

The Facts

Girls go through five different stages of puberty, and all of them are kick-started by hormones. Everybody has hormones, but some people's hormones start racing around earlier than others.

The Science Part

Basically, hormones are like little chemical messengers that carry a signal from one cell in your body to another. Hormones are made by glands and are released into your bloodstream. Hormones cause all kinds of changes in your body, many of which happen during puberty.

How It Starts

It begins by one of these hormones setting off on a journey to the pituitary gland, a pea-sized gland that sits at the base of your brain. When the hormone arrives, it jump-starts the pituitary gland into releasing two more hormones into your body.

brain

pituitary gland

Girls and Boys

Girls and boys have the same hormones in their body, but sometimes they go to different places and cause different things to happen. In girls, some hormones zoom from the pituitary gland to the female reproductive system, so they can make a girl's body ready for having babies if she chooses to when she's older.

The Five Stages of Puberty: What Happens and When Will It Begin?

Stage 1 could start any time between 8 and 11 years old. You can't see the signs on your body because it's all going on inside it. Hormones are starting to be made, and your ovaries (the parts of your body that hold tiny eggs, which might one day become babies) are getting bigger.

Stage 2 starts anytime from 8 to 14 years old, but usually sometime around the age of 12. Your breasts will begin to grow, you'll start to get taller and heavier, and hair will start to grow under your arms and between your legs. Near your vagina, the hair is called pubic hair.

Stage 3 can occur from 10 to 15 years old, but usually at 12 or 13. Your breasts will continue to grow, your hips will become wider, and any pubic hair will begin to get thicker. You may notice a clear or whitish discharge from your vagina (you might see this in your underwear). This isn't something to worry about—it's the way your body cleans itself naturally. Some girls may have their first period during this stage.

☆ **stage 4** happens anytime from 10 to 16 years old, but generally around 13 or 14. You will probably grow more pubic hair and the hair under your arms will get thicker. You will become fertile (able to have a baby) because your ovaries will start releasing eggs into the womb and you will begin having periods. Your breasts may become more defined in shape, and the dark skin around your nipples (the areolas) will probably get darker.

stage 5 usually occurs from 14 to 19 years old. Your breasts and pubic hair may be fully grown and you'll probably have reached your adult height. Your voice may have become a little deeper, your periods may have started to follow a regular pattern, and you will ovulate (release an egg) midway between each period. By this stage you'll almost be a fully grown woman—hurrah! But you don't have to deal with everything older women do—there's plenty of time for having fun!

Head Start

By the time you were six, your brain was already about 95 percent of its adult size. Now that you are becoming an adolescent (someone going through puberty), it is having a final growth spurt and a dramatic development into adulthood.

In girls, brain growth will probably get fast at 11 years old (in boys it's a bit later—typical!). Your brain will always be capable of learning new skills. But during puberty, the different parts of your brain get even better at helping you think and figure things out.

It's a little bit of an information overload at first, before the brain starts to put itself in order. But, by the end of puberty, your brain will have organized itself and work even better—the human brain is the best computer ever!

Which Side Are You On?

If you are good at math, writing, languages, and science, and are very logical, the left side of your brain is probably the dominant one. If you are good at music, art, and dance, and are very perceptive, the right side of your brain is probably the dominant one.

Left Side of Brain

right hand and right body side

good with numbers

good at getting things in order

language

Right Side of Brain

left hand and left body side

recognizing faces

tone of voice

good with shapes and movement

emotions and humor

Swing High, Swing Low

It's not surprising that adolescence is a time when you experience strong and changing emotions. Until now, you had feelings like being happy or sad, liking or disliking things. Now it probably feels like all those feelings have doubled. Sometimes you feel like a full-grown adult, ready to take on the world. At other times you might want to go back to being a little kid.

When you feel sad, you might feel like crying, sometimes for no good reason, and as if you are never going to smile again. Even when you are feeling like this, remember there are people you can talk to. Grown-ups, especially women, will know how you are feeling, and just talking about how you feel can help.

Quick Changes

Not only are your emotions stronger now, you've probably noticed that they change—really quickly! You might be happy playing with your baby brother one minute, then suddenly want to rush to your room and listen to music. It's just as confusing for you as it is for everyone else!

Let's Face It

One of the first signs of becoming a teenager is changes to your skin, especially on your face. This is because hormones make your skin more oily. Suddenly, your clear skin might become greasy, zitty, and bumpy. This is because the oil blocks the tiny holes in your skin (these holes are called pores) and makes zits appear. The zits can be itchy, burning, and sore.

Skin Sense

Your skin can change in different ways. You might have dry patches, an oily nose, and a bumpy forehead. Sometimes one at a time, and sometimes all together! So...

- Try not to touch your face with dirty fingers. Wash your hands before touching your face—and afterward!
- Make sure you clean any oil off glasses and sunglasses, or they might clog up your pores when you wear them.
- Don't squeeze zits! This could cause an infection, make the zits worse, and even scar your skin later on.
- Keep your skin clean and use makeup that is less likely to block your pores—if in doubt, ask in the drugstore or ask an adult you trust.

Clean and Clear!

Because your skin is working overtime, you'll need to start caring for it more thoroughly than before. Keeping your skin clean can reduce the amount of oil and soothe zits. What are the best ways of doing this? Well, we thought you'd never ask...

★ Use a mild cleanser in the morning and at bedtime, but don't scrub your skin too hard, or you could make it sore. Always remember to clean under your bangs.

★ Next, use a light, oil-free moisturizer, preferably with a Sun Protection Factor (SPF) of at least 20—as the skin on your face is very sensitive to damage from sunlight.

★ If you have zits, you can treat them with a lotion from the pharmacy. But BE CAREFUL! Some products are very strong and may irritate your skin.

★ If you wear makeup, always make sure you take it off before going to bed. Use a cleanser specially made for taking off makeup.

Myth Buster!
Teenage zits aren't caused by eating too much chocolate or sweet things.

Top Tip!
Wash towels and your pillowcase regularly.

11

A Bumpy Ride

Annoyingly, there are many different types of breakouts (sometimes called "zits" or "pimples") that can crop up on your face and body. Pimples, zits—whatever they are called, they can be a real drag! Everyone gets them, but some people just seem to sail through. How you look can make you feel really down, but pimples do go away... eventually! If you feel really low, talk to a friend, who will almost certainly have the same worries.

Acne is an inflammation of the skin and will probably be a mixture of blackheads and whiteheads. It appears mostly on the face, but can also develop on other parts of your body. Your skin might be red, sensitive to touch, and itchy. Some treatments from the drugstore can help reduce acne. But if it is really bad, visit your dermatologist. Most teens will get some form of acne during puberty.

Zit Tip

If you feel self-conscious about your zits, you can use a concealer a shade close to your skin tone to cover up the worst. This is usually quite thick in consistency, and contains an antiseptic that helps stop infection. Don't apply the concealer directly from the container, and always read the instructions. As a general method, place a small amount of concealer on a pad or the clean tip of your finger, then dab the concealer gently on the pimples, blending into the skin. And clean it off before you go to bed at night!

Blackheads are blackish or yellowish in color, and look like bumps in the skin. The black part isn't dirt, but the skin's own pigment, melanin, reacting with the air. They tend to take a while to go away.

Whiteheads are bumps on the skin that are whitish on the surface, because the pore underneath is completely blocked. These tend to go away more quickly than blackheads.

Freckles are harmless little brown spots on the skin. They're just little groups of pigment cells (cells that contain color). Freckles are usually flat, brown patches of skin that sometimes overlap. Not everyone likes their freckles, and there's no magic potion to make them go away, but using sun protection and keeping out of harsh sunlight may stop you from getting more. Lots of people think that freckles make a girl more beautiful!

The Agony of Acne

At some stage everyone gets worried about their appearance. You wouldn't like to get teased about something that already makes you feel uncomfortable, and no one else does either! So if you see someone with pimples or freckles, don't make fun of them. It isn't their fault!

A Hair-raising Story

OK, so you've had hair on your head for as long as you can remember. But when puberty starts, it might seem as if hair is sprouting everywhere on your body—sometimes in places you wish it wouldn't.

Remember we said that pubic hair grows near your vagina and *between* your legs? Well, you'll also grow hair on other parts of your body, in fact almost everywhere except on the palms of your hands and the soles of your feet. This is just normal body hair—but it isn't pubic hair.

Bearded Lady?

Before you start worrying that you might grow a beard, relax! Look at the grown-up women you know—mom, aunts, teachers, whoever. They all have tiny, fine hairs on their face, and yours won't be any different.

Worried?

Like everyone at some stage, you are going to feel great about the changes, and at other times they can be a drag. Remember, there are plenty of grown-ups who know just how it feels to be changing, and if there's anything worrying you, you can always talk to someone.

Sniff Sniff!

Your body uses hair as a way of attracting a mate. Your hair retains its own unique scent and, without any of us even realizing it, this scent is passed on to others via chemicals called pheromones. This smell attracts others to you—you could call it a dating service!

Handy Hair

Body hair is important! The hair on your body has lots of different uses—it's not just there to annoy you, though it may feel that way sometimes. It protects your skin from dirt and germs. It cushions the sensitive parts of your body by allowing less friction between your skin and your clothes. Hair also helps you stay warm in cold weather.

A Hairy Evolution

Millions of years ago, when humans didn't look the way we look now, our bodies were covered with much more hair. In cold weather, the little muscles at the base of each hair would work to make the hair stand on end. This made little pockets of air, which trapped heat. Even though we don't have enough hair for this to be useful anymore, it still happens. This is why your hair stands up when you're cold, and the little muscles working under your skin make goose bumps.

Myth Buster!

If you have dark hair, it may seem as though you've got more hair than your friends who are blondes or redheads. But dark hair is just a bit thicker, and can be seen more easily—it doesn't mean you're hairier than they are.

Changes You Can Expect
Between the ages of 8 and 16, the hair you already have on your body will start growing thicker, and new hair will appear.

So what will happen to you—and where and when? You will probably notice hair growing under your armpits first. Your eyebrows may get thicker and darker. A few hairs might start growing on your upper lip, and sometimes around your nipples or between your breasts.

Your legs will also start to grow hair, with more hair growing below the knees than on your thighs. Hair will start to grow on your genital area, too. As you get older, your pubic hair will become darker and coarser and will probably form a triangle shape. There's no way of telling the exact age that all these things will happen to you. These changes will develop when the time is right for you.

Keep It Cool
Every girl will go through these changes at different times. There is no "right" age, and it isn't a competition!

Q: I don't like all this hair that's growing on my body. How can I get rid of it?

A: Many women are happy with their body hair, but, if it makes you feel uncomfortable, there are ways you can remove it. Remember, it's a good idea to talk to a woman you trust before trying any of these suggestions yourself.

Q: Will it hurt to remove my hair?

A: Some methods of hair removal can be painful, but others are completely painless. What's most important is that it's done properly, and that you get advice first.

Shaving

For underarms and legs. Make sure you use a razor designed for girls, and that the blades are clean and sharp. Use shaving gel or foam to soften the skin beforehand.

Waxing

For any body hair. This is best done at a beauty salon and can be painful. Wax is applied to the skin and then pulled off with a strip of paper or fabric.

Plucking

For eyebrows. Hairs are plucked out one at a time with a pair of tweezers. You could ask someone else do it the first time, and use the eyebrow shape they create as a guide to follow.

Depilatory

For legs and underarms. A hair-removing cream is applied to the hair, left on for a set time, and then removed promptly. Always follow the product's instructions carefully.

Pubic Hair

Everyone is different and has their own opinion; some girls and women like their pubic hair just the way it is, and some like to trim their pubic hair (carefully, with a small pair of scissors) so that it doesn't show outside their underwear or bathing suit. Some like to shave or wax the edges, and some prefer to remove all their pubic hair. The choice is yours!

Bad Hair Day

Each hair on your head has three layers, with a cuticle layer on the outside for protection against sunlight and pollution.

Shiny hair is a sign of good health—it shows that the cuticle layers are lying flat and reflecting the light. The hair follicles on your head contain *sebaceous glands*, which make *sebum*—just like the oily *sebum* your skin produces. During puberty, you may find that your hair gets greasier as the *sebaceous glands* get busier.

Twists and Turns

Straighter hair can look shinier than curly hair, but this doesn't mean curly hair isn't beautiful hair. It just reflects the light differently. If you have got very curly hair, you may want to make sure that it is well nourished and conditioned to increase its shine.

All Washed Up

If you find you have very oily hair, you may want to wash it every day. It's OK to wash it more often as long as you use a mild shampoo. Using too many harsh chemicals can damage your hair and irritate the scalp. Try using a baby shampoo instead.

Turn down the heat

Heat-styling products, like hair dryers and straighteners, can cause damage to your hair, so use them carefully and try to give your hair time out occasionally. You could also use a heat-styling product to help protect your hair.

Chemical treatments

Things like hair dye and relaxers can also do lots of damage to hair. If you do use them, follow the instructions carefully or, better still, go to a salon for professional treatment.

Dandruff

If you have dandruff (dry, white flakes of skin in your hair), resist scratching your scalp and use an anti-dandruff shampoo. Dandruff is not contagious! Remember, if you don't rinse your hair thoroughly, dry bits of conditioner, shampoo or other hair products can look like dandruff.

Nit picking

Catching headlice can be quite common when you're younger. Remember, if someone has headlice, it's not because they are dirty. In fact, headlice prefer clean hair! Headlice are almost invisible insects that grip onto your hair. They feed on your blood by biting your scalp – nice! They also produce sticky white eggs (called nits) that stick to your hair.

To get rid of headlice and nits you can use a special shampoo or lotion from the chemist. You'll need to carefully follow the instructions on the packet and then get someone to comb through your hair to remove the dead lice and eggs.

The Booby Prize

The appearance of "breast buds" (swellings that show that your breasts are starting to grow) can be the first sign of puberty. They can appear as young as 7 years old or maybe not until 13, and it takes about 5 or 6 years for your breasts to reach their full size. Your breasts grow at different rates, so don't be surprised or worried if one looks slightly larger than the other.

Women have breasts so they are able to produce breast milk for their babies. Breasts are made up of milk glands, ducts, and other body tissues. Breast size has a lot to do with your family: if your mom is tall, you might be tall; if she has small breasts, yours may also be small—but there are no guarantees!

Little or Large?

There's not much you can do to change the size of your breasts. You've probably heard of celebrities who have "boob jobs" to make their breasts bigger, but that kind of operation costs LOADS of money and is very painful. It's much better to be happy with who you are, no matter what your bra size is.

Q: What if I feel a lump in my breast?
A: As your breasts grow, they can feel lumpy, especially before a period. It's a good idea to get into the habit of checking your breats for lumps every month or so. If you notice a change or a lump, talk to a trusted adult. It's always better to go to a doctor to get it checked out. If something is wrong they can take care of it, and your mind will be put at rest.

Q: What if my breasts look different from other girls' breasts?
A: Breasts come in all shapes and sizes: large nipples, small nipples, inverted ones (sticking in, not out), ones that point up, down, or to the side, dark ones, light ones... Everyone is different!

Q: My breasts are sore! Is this normal?
A: Yes! It's normal for developing breast buds to be tender and even itchy as they grow. Wearing a bra may help by protecting them.

First Bras

There are no rules as to when you should get your first bra. The time is probably right when you feel self-conscious about your breasts. Bra sizes are based on two measurements: one is the distance around your rib cage just below your breasts, the second is around your rib cage in line with your nipples. Bras come in many different sizes to fit these measurements.

Bravissimo!

Bras come in all kinds of styles. A sports style might be good as a first bra, or you might prefer one with a little padding. Buy at least two bras so you can allow time for washing and drying them.

Fitting In

Don't feel embarrassed about being fitted for your first bra. You'll probably want an adult to go with you, so talk to her first at home. The woman in the store has fitted hundreds of girls. You'll go into a private fitting room to be measured—it won't be done in the middle of the store!

The Wonderful World of Periods

You will probably start your periods ("menstruate" is the scientific name) about two years after your breasts begin to grow. For a lot of girls, this is between the ages of 10 and 14.

You are born with two ovaries, both containing tiny eggs, which have the potential to become babies. Puberty prompts the first egg to leave one of the ovaries and travel down the Fallopian tube to the uterus (also known as the womb). The same hormones that ripened the egg thicken the lining of your womb. If the egg isn't fertilized, the lining of the womb breaks down and your period will start!

What Will Happen?

When you get your period, your uterus will discharge its lining (blood and other stuff) from your vagina. It lasts a few days (or maybe a week), and you will lose only a few tablespoons of blood. The discharge could range from dark brown to bright red, and it might be fairly thick or runny.

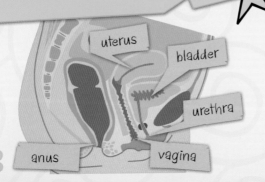

uterus
bladder
urethra
anus
vagina

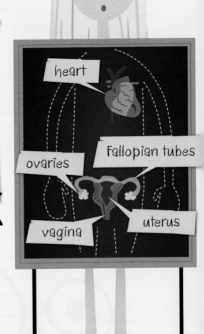

heart
Fallopian tubes
ovaries
vagina
uterus

A Long Way to Go

Most women have periods from their teens until menopause (when their periods stop) about the age of 45-55.

Period Patterns

You might have your first period and then not have another for a few months. But at some stage the timing of your periods will form a pattern known as a cycle. Each cycle lasts about 28 days and ends when you have a period, which lasts about 3-5 days.

Pregnant Pause!

Even if a girl hasn't started having periods yet, she can still get pregnant. Remember that the egg is released by the ovary **before** the period comes, so it can still be fertilized in the womb—even if it's the very first egg!

Top Tip!

Holding a hot-water bottle or warming pad over your tummy can help ease a sore or cramped stomach during your period.

That Time of the Month

Every girl will feel differently about her periods. Some girls aren't bothered by them at all, others can feel a bit grouchy or emotional before their period. This is known as PMS (which stands for premenstrual syndrome). Here are some things you might experience:

- ♥ You might get tired more easily before and during your period.
- ♥ Your breasts might feel tender or sore before or during your period.
- ♥ Your stomach might feel bloated or a little achy.
- ♥ Some girls get cramplike pains in their abdomen at the beginning.

Napkins and Tampons

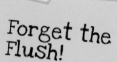

Sanitary napkins are thin pads that you attach to your underwear.

- They come in different sizes and soak up different amounts of blood.
- They need to be changed every few hours during the day.
- You can't wear a napkin while swimming.

Tampons are like rolls of cotton with a string attached to one end. Tampons are inserted into the vagina, where they can soak up the blood, and are removed by gently pulling the string, which stays outside the vagina.

- They are usually used by older girls.
- They are ideal if you play a lot of sports.

Forget the Flush!

Dispose of used napkins and tampons in the trash at home, and in the special bins at school or in public restrooms. Never flush them down a toilet!

Most Important

Tampons MUST be changed every few hours and should NEVER be left in the vagina for longer than eight hours. If you do, in rare cases, girls can develop something called Toxic Shock Syndrome, which will need urgent medical treatment.

Squeaky Clean

You may notice a clear, creamy, white, or slightly yellowy discharge in your underwear. This is how your vagina keeps itself clean and healthy. If you notice a change or are worried, talk to an adult you trust.

Q&A

Q: What should I do if my period starts at school?

A: Tell the school nurse or your favorite female teacher. They will probably have some pads for you to use. Don't be embarrassed—it happens to lots of girls! In an absolute emergency, you can always make a wad of toilet paper to place inside your underpants. Even if your periods haven't started, it's a good idea to buy some napkins so you are well prepared.

Baby Talk

A woman is fertile (able to get pregnant) when an egg leaves the ovary and begins its journey to the uterus. When a man and a woman have sex, semen is passed out of his penis into the woman's vagina. The sperm swim into the woman's uterus, and if one comes into contact with the egg, the woman can get pregnant. Sex should only happen between two people who care for each other, have discussed it first, and are sure it's what they want. A woman shouldn't have sex because:

● Someone is pressuring her to.
● Other people say they have (most people haven't before they are 16).
● She thinks it will make her more mature.
● She thinks it will make someone like her more.

Contraception

To stop a woman from getting pregnant, contraception can be used. Some types of contraception can also protect against STIs (Sexually Transmitted Infections), which are diseases men and women can catch from each other by having sex. The only 100 percent effective way of not getting pregnant or an STI is not to have sex.

Slow Down!

There's no rush for a girl to start having boyfriends and thinking about kissing, cuddling, or even getting too involved. There are so many other exciting things to do in life. It's best to leave serious stuff like that to the adults, don't you think?

Remember...

If someone has ever done anything physical to you that makes you feel uncomfortable, you must talk to an adult you can trust—maybe a teacher. It isn't your fault, and no one will be angry with you for telling the truth.

A Weight Off Your Mind

During puberty your body gets taller and heavier as it builds up muscle and fat, which makes older women stronger and curvier. As teens, girls might gain more weight than boys—this is normal because girls' bodies are preparing for possibly having babies one day.

Because you are growing up and burning lots of energy doing it, you might feel hungrier than ever! As long as you eat a balance of healthy foods and a few treats, and exercise, your weight gain should be just right. No matter what size or shape you are, remember that there are over 6 billion people on the planet, and you are the only you in the whole world—you are special and gorgeous!

One of a Kind! Girls of the same age can be all different shapes and sizes. Remember, it's our differences that make us beautiful!

A varied diet is a healthy one. Make sure you:

- Have between three and five portions of fruits and vegetables a day—this can include fruit juice.
- Make about a third of your diet starchy foods like bread, cereals, rice, pasta, and potatoes. They provide energy, fiber, calcium, iron, and B vitamins.
- Don't eat too much fat and sugar—so not too many cookies, cakes, chips, or things like butter, cheese, ice cream and hot dogs.
- If you are a meat-eater, choose meats like chicken and turkey, and eat fish, including at least one portion of oily fish, like salmon, per week.

Rise and Shine!

Always make time in the morning to eat breakfast. It will give you an energy boost to help you concentrate at school, and will keep you from feeling hungry before lunchtime.

H2 Oh!

If you are thirsty, drink water instead of sugary drinks or sodas. Drink regularly during the day —don't wait until you're thirsty! Most schools allow people to drink water during classes. If your school hasn't caught up yet, maybe you could raise the subject with the PTA.

Salty Snacks

Watch how much salt you have—not just what you put on food yourself! Fast food and chips often have lots of salt in them. Always try to read labels on food—you shouldn't have more than 6g of sodium a day.

You Are What You Eat!

Eating healthily may seem like a big challenge, especially when there's so much tempting junk food around and you feel hungry all the time because you're growing so much! But it's an important habit to get into... for life.

Your school should provide well-balanced lunches and lots of fruit for snacks, but when you're not at school, it's up to you—make sure you keep up the good work at home!

Q&A

Q: Why should I eat healthy food?
A: It will make you feel better and look better. A balanced diet that includes vitamins and minerals will give you shinier hair and stronger nails and teeth. You should also find that good food puts you in a better mood, and helps you play, sing, dance, and breathe better. It helps you concentrate better at school, too!

Q: So what if I am bigger than my friends? I like the way I am!
A: You're right—we don't all need to look identical. But if you are really overweight, you might find that there are disadvantages:

★ You might not enjoy taking part in sports because it is harder work to run and keep up with others.
★ Some really overweight people can become ill with diabetes or high blood pressure.

Q: Being healthy sounds great! What should I do?
A: Here are some simple rules:
★ Eat a balance of healthy food and occasional treats
★ Exercise regularly
★ Drink lots of water

Body Mass Index (BMI) is a way to work out if you are a healthy weight for your height. You can find a BMI calculator on the Internet. If your BMI indicates that you are a healthy weight, this means you are – it doesn't lie! If you are still worried about your weight, speak to a doctor or an adult you trust.

Eating disorders

The best thing about food is enjoying eating it. But sometimes, people can get hung up about food. Some eat too much and don't exercise, others eat too little and lose weight. Both are equally dangerous to your health. Anorexia nervosa and bulimia nervosa are two eating disorders that girls and boys can get when they become too concerned about what they eat and how much they exercise. This happens to very, very few young people, but if you are worried that someone you know has an eating disorder, it's very important to speak to an adult and let them know.

The Eyes Have It

Your eyes are your windows onto the world, so you'll want to do everything you can to keep them healthy. Even if you don't need glasses, you still have to look after those precious eyeballs!

Here's how to keep those peepers in top-notch condition:

- ♥ Eat a healthy diet and drink lots of water.
- ♥ Exercise regularly. Eyes need oxygen to stay healthy, and exercise will increase the oxygen supply in your body.
- ♥ Make sure you get enough sleep.
- ♥ Wear sunglasses in the summer and goggles if you go skiing, to protect against damage from UV rays.
- ♥ Have regular checkups with your eye doctor.
- ♥ If you need glasses, wear them. If you don't, your eyes will get tired and sore. You also won't be able to see things properly and could fall behind at school.

Classy Glassy

Glasses come in so many styles! Some people need them for reading books (farsighted), and some people need them for watching TV (nearsighted). Making fun of someone who wears glasses is a dumb thing to do.

How to take care of your glasses:

♥ Keep your glasses in their case when you aren't wearing them.

♥ Keep them clean, using a lens cloth or cleaner.

♥ You can get prescription goggles to wear when swimming if you need them.

♥ If you play a lot of sports, choose a pair of flexible glasses or get a band that attaches to your glasses and keeps them on your head.

Q&A

Q: I hate wearing glasses. Can I wear contact lenses?
A: You need to ask your eye doctor for advice. The most important thing about contacts is taking care of them. An optometrist may recommend contact lenses that are used once and thrown away. If contact lenses aren't kept clean and sterile, they can damage the health of your eyes.

The good things about contact lenses are:

★ No one knows you are wearing them.

★ They are easier to cope with if you do a lot of outdoor sports.

The downside of contact lenses is that:

★ They can be expensive.

★ If they're not disposable ones, you need to be careful to clean them properly.

★ You can only wear certain kinds for swimming.

★ They can take some time to get used to.

★ Not everyone can wear contacts.

Pearly Whites

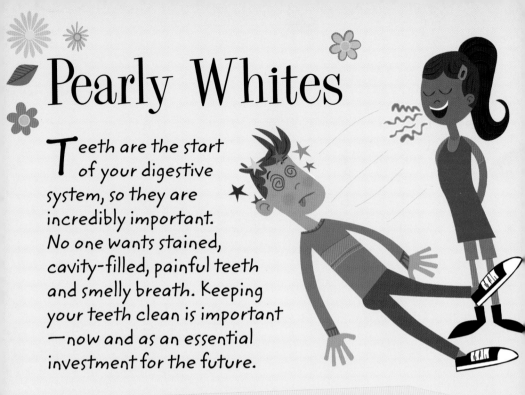

Teeth are the start of your digestive system, so they are incredibly important. No one wants stained, cavity-filled, painful teeth and smelly breath. Keeping your teeth clean is important —now and as an essential investment for the future.

How to Keep Your Teeth Clean:

- Brush twice a day with a fluoride toothpaste and soft toothbrush. Brush in small circles, not up and down or across, for about two minutes.
- Clean between your teeth with floss once a day, preferably before bedtime.
- Visit your dentist twice a year.
- Limit the amount of soda and sugary snacks you consume. It's better to sip drinks through a straw to avoid coating your teeth with sugar.

Pearls of Wisdom

You will have most of your adult teeth by the time you are 13 or 14. But the last teeth to arrive in your mouth are your wisdom teeth, or third molars, which will appear sometime after you are 17. You might not have room in your mouth for wisdom teeth to grow properly. Your dentist or orthodontist will keep a close eye on their progress and make suggestions for treatment if necessary.

Close Contact

If you play any kind of contact sport (such as field hockey, soccer, or basketball) always wear protection for your teeth. A mouthguard can prevent broken teeth and damage to your gums. You can buy one at a sporting goods store and follow the instructions to make it fit your own mouth. You can also have one made by your dentist. It will be more expensive, but it will fit perfectly and can also be made in your favorite color!

Brace Yourself

If your teeth are crooked or overcrowded, or your upper and lower jaws don't bite together properly, your dentist might recommend that you wear braces. An orthodontist specializes in fitting braces, and treatment can last from a few months to three years. You might be fitted with a clear plastic brace or have metal brackets fitted to individual teeth, which are linked with thin wires or elastic links.

Braces are like magnets for food! Make sure you follow your orthodontist's advice about keeping them and your teeth clean, such as using an alcohol-free mouthwash once a day. After all, there's no point to having lovely straight teeth if they are all decayed! Braces won't last forever, and they will have benefits for the rest of your life.

Bad Breath is caused by poor dental hygiene, smoking, some foods, or even a medical problem. Cleaning your teeth and tongue regularly can usually clear the stink up for most girls. If it doesn't, ask your dentist for advice.

Hot Tip! Don't brush your teeth right after drinking soda or orange juice—this could soften the hard outer layer of your teeth (the enamel). Instead, rinse your mouth with water and wait 30 minutes before brushing.

Best Foot Forward

Your feet are often the first part of your body to have a growth spurt during puberty. You may find they get two or three sizes bigger in a short space of time. Feet tend to stop growing about a year before you reach your final height and, with girls, your feet may reach their full size when you're about 14.

Stinky Feet!

Your feet have lots of glands that release a fluid containing salt and water—in other words, sweat! If you don't wash your feet regularly and give them a rest from being confined to shoes, the bacteria on your skin will attack the sweat and start to smell.

If you want to avoid frightfully foul feet:
- ♥ Wash your feet every day, with soap and water, in the shower or bath.
- ♥ Dry your feet thoroughly after washing.
- ♥ Keep your toenails clean and short.
- ♥ Wear well-ventilated shoes or ones made of leather.
- ♥ Don't wear sneakers all the time or the same pair of shoes every day.

Wicked Warts

Plantar warts are just ordinary warts, which anyone can get, but because they are on the soles of your feet, they grow inward and look different from a wart that you might get on your hand. WARTS ARE CONTAGIOUS. This means that you can catch them from other people. The most common places to catch warts are swimming pools and locker rooms. Although they are not harmful, they can be uncomfortable and do need to be treated.

Hot Tip!
Avoid catching warts or spreading them by wearing special swim shoes. You can buy these at sporting goods stores, drugstores, or at your local pool. Try not to share shoes or socks, and avoid direct contact with warts on other parts of the body or on other people. Treat warts by following the advice of your doctor or pharmacist. If they are really bad or painful, see a podiatrist—this is a doctor who specializes in foot care.

Fashion Frenzy

Not many girls can resist the lure of trendy footwear, but fashionable shoes are not always comfortable. High heels force all your weight painfully onto the front of your feet, making you unsteady and risking injury. Tight-fitting shoes can cause corns (lumps of hard skin) and blisters (sore swellings). Long-term wear of high heels can even cause back, tendon, and knee problems. To avoid terrible toe trauma:

★ Wear low-heeled shoes for everyday and save fashion shoes for weekends and parties.

★ Go barefoot when you are at home to give your feet a rest.

★ Try wearing heels that also have a platform sole—they'll balance your weight more evenly.

Clean Up Your Act

*E*veryone perspires (that's "sweating" to you and me). It's a perfectly normal thing throughout adult life. We sweat so that we don't overheat. Everyone has —gulp—about 3 million (yes, million!) sweat glands on their body. And when puberty starts, they all become more active. Some girls get worried about sweating, but it's just the body's natural way of cooling off.

Everyone has natural oil (called sebum) on their skin. It keeps your skin moist and waterproof. And during puberty you'll probably have more of it in certain places. Another thing we all have is dead skin. Though you can't see it happening, every minute of the day we lose about 30,000 to 40,000 dead skin cells from the surface of our skin! When bacteria joins the mix, the body can start to smell.

Sniff, Sniff!

It's not always possible to smell your own sweat, but it can be really noticeable to other people. (Just imagine the stench in the locker room at school when a lot of people have been in there on a hot day, changing after PE.) It's better to get into a routine of washing regularly and not wait for someone to tell you you've got body odor (BO).

Q: How do I make sure I don't smell —or get rid of it when I do?

A: Wash every day, preferably in the shower or bath.

★ Use an antiperspirant deodorant to prevent your armpits from smelling. Don't just spray deodorant onto unwashed armpits. The sweet smell will only mingle with the sweat!

★ Don't spray deodorant onto your clothes. It will only stain or damage them, and it won't stop you from sweating or smelling!

★ Change your shirt or top, underpants, and socks or pantyhose daily, and your bra every few days.

Q: I play a lot of sports so get really sweaty! How do I keep the smell under control?

A: Make sure you take a shower after sports, and dry your body thoroughly afterward. And put fresh clothes on, too—there's no point in washing off the sweaty smell only to put sweaty clothes back on!

Q: My school has a uniform, and I wear the same one every day. How do I keep it smelling fresh?

A: If you wear a school uniform, change out of it when you get home and hang it up to let it air. It's also important to have more than one shirt so you can wear a clean one every day.

Myth Buster!

It's fine to take a bath or shower during your period. Never try to clean inside your vagina, and avoid using very highly perfumed soaps, because they can make your vagina itchy and sore.

Hot Tip!
Hang your towel up to dry after use. If you leave it in a pile on the floor, it will start to smell. If you leave it in a pile on your bed, it will not only smell but it will make your bed wet, too! Use a fresh, clean towel every two or three days.

✩All in the Family

M ost kids get along well with their parents or caregivers. You take it for granted that they are always there for you. But when you reach your teens, you'll want to start making more decisions for yourself—and your folks at home might not be ready for that.

OK, so you used to like shopping for clothes with your mom. Now, you might think you wouldn't be seen dead shopping with her, and the clothes she likes are so babyish! And your dad might think you shouldn't stay up so late, or might start telling you to turn your music down or not to spend so much time on the Internet. It's hard to imagine, but your mom and dad used to feel just like you when they were your age!

And maybe you used to enjoy hanging out with your brothers and sisters. Now their baby games are driving you nuts! And the older ones always want to tell you what to do. You just want your own space!

Remember: puberty is when your parents start acting weird!

Coping with Family Conflict

One minute you want to be treated like an independent adult. Next, you just want to be a child again. Here are some ideas for how to cope with your changing family relationships:

♥ Talk with your parents about how you feel. Ask if they can let you have more privacy.

♥ Don't keep friends secret. Bring them home.

♥ Try not to be in a rush about growing up.

♥ If you want to be treated like an adult, try not to lose your temper all the time like a child throwing a tantrum.

♥ They want your room straightened up now, but you want to do it later —can you compromise? A little give and take can go a long way!

♥ When you go out, tell them where you are going to be, and if you agree on a time to be home—be back on time. Remember, it's not that they don't want you to have a good time or don't trust you, they just worry about you because they love you so much. It will take them time to know for sure that you will be safe.

Strange but True
Obviously, your friends' parents are much cooler than your own. The weird thing is, your friends probably think your parents rock!

Oldies but Goodies
Having you as a teenager is probably making your parents feel really, really old— poor old things!

Crazy Crushes

During puberty, you might start to notice boys in a different way. It's normal to develop exciting feelings about other people. It's fine to think all kinds of romantic thoughts about how much you'd love to be with that person. Just remember that fantasies are fine, but you also have to deal with boring things like going to school and brushing your teeth!

Q&A

Q: Why does everyone keep talking about this boy? I just don't get it.
A: It's OK not to like the same things as your friends. You can still be pals even if you have different tastes in music, clothes, and boys.

Q: I think I love him! But he always ignores me—how can I get him to notice me?
A: Maybe this boy hasn't started to think about girls in that way yet. Try to spark a friendship by talking about your common interests. Or you could ask a friend to tell the boy that you like him! Be yourself. If he never notices you, that's his loss! And if he does, you don't have to do everything he says or asks—YOU decide what's right for you.

Q: Lately I've started to have feelings for another girl. Aren't I supposed to only like boys?
A: Loads of kids have same-sex crushes during puberty —they just might not admit it! Everyone has their own preferences—some girls like boys with dark hair, some girls like boys with blond hair, and some girls like girls! If, when you are older, you still like girls, that's absolutely fine, too.

That Crushing Feeling ⭐

Suddenly you've become obsessed with someone. It could be a boy or girl at school or on your street, a male or female teacher, or even a celebrity. You can't stop thinking about them. You go out of your way to be in the same place they are. But when you are near them, you often feel tongue-tied and silly. It sounds like you've got a crush on someone.

When you've got a crush, the intense feelings might seem like they're taking over your life. Try not to let that happen. Just as your feelings about everything else are strong and changeable, the chances are you will change your mind about your crush in a few months anyway. No matter how strong your emotions are, remember that experiencing these feelings about people is a way of finding out the kind of people you like.

You're Not the Only One! Most of us get crushes at some time or another— even adults!

Friends Are for Life
It can be tricky when all you can think about is your crush, but don't forget to keep in touch with your friends. They've stuck by you through good times and bad, and deserve your loyalty.

School Daze

You probably don't like all the teachers and subjects, and sometimes when you're at school, work is the last thing on your mind. But school is where you spend a lot of your time, so it's a good idea to try and enjoy it.

Q&A

Q: I'm worried that I'm not popular.
A: You've got friends—of course you are popular with some people. No one is universally loved by everyone. Be yourself and your friends will always be there for you.

Q: Everyone else is smarter than me—it's not fair! How can I get smarter?
A: We're all good at some things, and very few people are brilliant at everything. Just make sure you concentrate in class and do all the homework you are given. If you don't understand something, speak to your teacher and tell them how you feel. They will want to help.

Beating the Bullies
Bullies don't just use physical strength to put people down. They do it by calling them names (either to their face or behind their backs), or by excluding them from friendship groups. Your school will have ways of dealing with bullying. If you are being bullied, or if you think someone else is, speak to a teacher you trust who will help you.

Peer Pressure

As you grow up, you'll have all kinds of exciting things to do, but also some things to be careful about. People might encourage you to skip school, smoke cigarettes, or take other drugs—how stupid is that? Some young people think that it's fine to drink alcohol, but it can be dangerous. Besides being illegal before the age of 21, drinking alcohol can lead to taking risks that you might later regret, and can seriously affect your health.

OK, so lots of people think that a little alcohol is fine for adults, but that's a decision for you to make when you're older. They are YOUR decisions. Doing something just because you think other people are doing it is kind of dumb, and letting other people decide what happens to you is really crazy!

Friendships should:
♥ Be fun
♥ Make you feel special
♥ Be reassuring and comfortable

They shouldn't:
♥ Be hard work
♥ Make you feel bad about yourself
♥ Tempt you to do things that you know are wrong or make you uncomfortable

Friend or Foe?
It's good to have lots of friends, but don't forget about your old ones when new ones come along. Some new friends might seem very exciting at first, and they might be great for you, but give it time to make sure they get to know you, you get to know them, and that you're good for each other. Don't let a new friend make you do something that you know isn't right.

Keeping in Touch

Mobile or cell phones and the Internet can be a lot of fun to use. But remember to think carefully about all the things you're getting into!

Having your own phone is a lifeline to independence, so don't risk losing it. Using your phone during school could get it confiscated. Don't use it if you've been told not to. Also, remember that your phone probably cost a lot of money, so you should treat it like any valuable object and take care of it—don't leave it in a stupid place or be clumsy with it.

Q&A

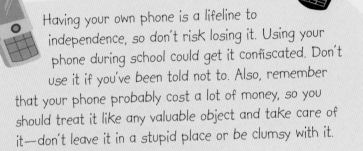

Q: My parents are always nagging at me to get off my phone. How can I get them off my back?

A: Just make sure you use your phone responsibly. Keep in touch with your parents while you're out with your friends. And make sure you stay within your monthly minutes. Your parents are probably the ones paying your phone bill, so they won't appreciate you being careless with the number of texts and calls you make. It's also a good idea to stay off your phone during mealtimes or when spending quality time with your family—they'd like your full attention!

Get the Message

Only give your phone number to people you know. If you receive a call or text from someone you don't know, don't respond. And tell an adult if anyone is hassling you via your phone, either with rude or upsetting messages or with pictures.

A Site for Sore Eyes

Social networking sites are a great way of keeping in touch with your friends when you aren't at school, or with friends you know from other places. But use your cyber sense.

Do:

★ Keep the group of friends you chat with exclusive.

★ Keep your profile locked and private. You don't want someone else changing stuff, even if they think they are just being funny.

★ Be careful who you give your email address to. Keep it private to avoid loads of junk mail.

★ Report people who are pestering you, or any worrying material, to the site monitors. If necessary, shut down your own section of the site.

★ Remember that other people can copy stuff you put online. Even if you have second thoughts and delete something, whatever you put on the Internet is there forever!

Don't:

✱ Put up photos or comments that might embarrass you or any of your friends.

✱ Allow your network to be accessed by people you don't know.

✱ Give anyone your password.

✱ Forget that teachers, colleges, and even future employers may check on social networking sites to see what you've been up to. What seemed funny last night might not be so clever tomorrow...

✱ Let someone coax you into saying or doing something online that you feel uncomfortable with. Never give details about yourself or send pictures to someone unless you are sure who they are.

Keep Your Cool

If someone writes something about you that you don't like, don't make horrible replies (and don't let someone else do it for you). Ask an adult you trust how to handle it and explain that you don't want to make things worse.

Glossary

adolescence / adolescent
The time in your life also known as puberty / someone who is going through puberty.

anorexia nervosa   An eating disorder characterized by the fear of becoming overweight, resulting in excessive dieting and exercising, and serious illness.

anus   The hole in your bottom where solid waste comes out when you go to the toilet.

bulimia nervosa   An eating disorder characterized by eating large amounts of food in short bursts, then vomiting afterwards. It can result in serious illness.

cervix   The entrance to the womb at the top of the vagina.

contraception   The general name for different ways to stop a woman becoming pregnant.

dandruff   Flakes of dead skin from your scalp.

discharge   Any fluid that leaks out of the human body but especially from the vagina.

Fallopian tubes   A pair of tubes leading from the ovaries to the womb.

follicles   Tiny holes in your skin where hairs grow.

gland   A cell or organ that makes chemical substances and then releases them into the body.

hormone   A chemical substance made by glands and then transported around the body.

menopause   The time when a woman's periods stop and she can no longer have a baby.

menstruation   The discharge of blood and other substances from the womb and out of the vagina.

oestrogen   A hormone, mainly produced by the ovaries, that develops the female body.

ovaries   The female reproductive organs which produce eggs, or ova.

ovulation   The release of eggs from the ovaries.

pituitary gland   A pea-sized gland that sits at the base of the brain and releases hormones.

puberty   The amazing process when a girl's body gradually changes to become a woman (and a boy's body changes to become a man).

pubic bone   A protective bone at the front of the pelvis.

pubic hair   Hair growing near your vagina and covering your pubic bone.

pubic hair   Hair growing near your vagina and covering your pubic bone.

sanitary napkin   A thin pad that fits in your underpants to soak up the discharge during a period.

sebum   The oily substance released by sebaceous glands onto hair and skin.

tampon   A small sausage-shaped roll of cotton, which is inserted into the vagina to absorb blood during a period.

vagina   The tube that leads from the cervix of the uterus to an outer opening, between the urethra and anus. It is very stretchy to allow a baby to come out.

urethra   A tiny tube that takes urine (pee) from the bladder to the outside of your body. The end of the urethra forms a small opening in your body just above the vagina.

uterus   A hollow organ lying within a woman's abdomen, in which a baby grows.

wart   a small painful lump on the skin, caused by a virus.

Index

Notes for Parents and Teachers

As adults, it's easy to forget how much children's minds, bodies, and social environment change in just a few years. These can be turbulent times for young people and their families and teachers. It can feel daunting, but this book is designed to help girls (although their brothers might also find it interesting) through the transformation from childhood into adulthood.

- Familiarize yourself with this book and learn when and how to describe the physical changes, adult emotions, or themes in a way that a child can understand.

- Try reading parts (or all) of this book together. It's a great way to start those conversations.

- If she prefers to read alone, leave the book available and then invite questions at a later time.

- Just talking to the girl in your care, taking an interest in her interests, praising conscientious behavior, and listening to what she says is all part of the process.

- Don't try to give all the information at once. Offer small amounts and invite her to question you.

- If you are male, be confident about offering your support to the girl in your care. You have an important role in influencing her health, well-being, and the way in which she comes to view the opposite sex.

- Teachers are incredibly important. Check that your school policy, which should be developed in consultation with parents and pupils, supports you teaching and answering questions. If it doesn't—update it!

The girls in our care will mirror the ways in which we treat them and treat each other. The personal relationships that we build with them can prepare them to deal with any difficult times they may face. They need and deserve a solid foundation of love and trust, based on honest, open communication.